Vicki Stiefel *presents*

CHEST OF BONE
THE KNIT COLLECTION

patterns from

Karen Clements • Norah Gaughan • Rosemary (Romi) Hill

Afterworld Publishing

www.vickistiefel.com
Burbank, Calif.

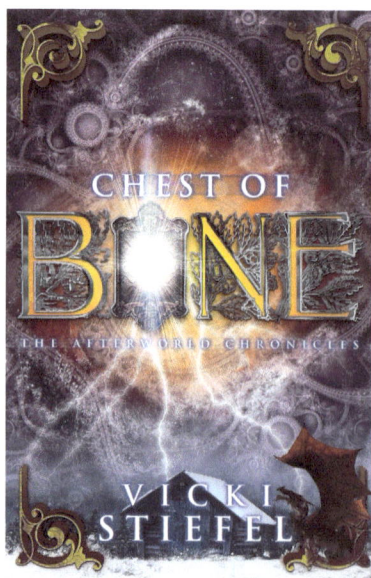

Welcome to *Chest of Bone: The Knit Collection*.

I'm so proud to present five evocative knitting patterns by iconic knitwear designers—Karen Clements, Norah Gaughan, and Rosemary (Romi) Hill—designs that reflect the world and the characters of my fantasy-suspense novel, *Chest of Bone*. The short story I've written for the collection, "A Very Special Project," is, indeed, a challenging one for my protagonist, Clea. We've also included brief character descriptions, and preview chapters from the novel.

How did this come about?

When I wrote *Chest of Bone*, I created a knitter as a protagonist. If vyou've read my book, *10 Secrets of the LaidBack Knitters* (with Lisa Souza), you know I'm passionate about knitting and knitters.

A knitter for a fantasy-suspense novel's hero? You betcha! Knitters are complex. They wear tattoos and pearls, are cops and homemakers and doctors, are grandfathers and teens and kids.

And so I invented Clea Reese because I delighted in a complex protagonist who adores knitting. Clea's also got a wicked sense of humor, a kickass attitude, and an unstoppable determination. Knitters deserve that complexity in a hero with whom they can identify.

Clea is many things—a talented empath and a magical Mage, an FBI special agent, and a woman bent on revenge. As well as a knitter, Clea is also raises cashmere goats, creatures she dearly loves.

When Clea's magic manifests with intention, her "fireflies" form knitting motifs, from Waterlilies to Tree-of-Life. Knitting connects to her magic and vice versa.

As my novel grew in pages, I imagined a pattern book to accompany it, so I reached out to Romi, Norah, and Karen. After reading the novel, each jumped onboard to create our knitting collection.

The collection—intended for a variety of skill levels, yarns, and gauges—reflects what the characters wear in the novel, as well as their personalities. We hope you enjoy it!

Come knit with us. Come knit with Clea.

Table of Contents

About the Designers and Author

Knitwear designer **Rosemary (Romi) Hill** lives on the eastern slope of the Sierra Nevada mountains in Northern Nevada, where the high desert nights are cool and the air is crisp. A lifelong crafter and knitter, she is inspired by the natural surroundings in her corner of the world, and her designs have an organic flow. Her work has appeared in publications such as *Vogue Knitting, Interweave Knits, Knitscene* and *Twist Collective*, and in numerous books. Romi's book *New Lace Knitting* was published in September 2015. She loves dark chocolate with chili peppers, and she's a sucker for a great pair of cowboy boots. See Romi's full pattern collection on Ravelry.

www.designsbyromi.com • *Ravelry*: designers/Rosemary-Romi-Hill
Facebook: RomiDesigns• *Instagram:* RomiDesigns •

Raised by artists in the Hudson Valley (her father, Jack Gaughan, was a well known science fiction illustrator in his day) **Norah Gaughan** was immersed in both art and the needle arts from an early age. Norah went on to earn a degree in Biology/Art from Brown University. During the years that followed she concentrated on her greatest love, knitting. First as a freelancer for yarn companies and knitting magazines, then as the design director at JCA, and more recently, as the design director at Berroco where she headed up the design team and published sixteen eponymous booklets. Norah's upbringing, schooling, and experience coalesce in her two hardcover volumes *Knitting Nature* and *Norah Gaughan's Knitted Cable Sourcebook*, both published by Abrams.

www.NorahGaughan.net • *Ravelry*: designers/Norah-Gaughan •
Facebook: norahsgaughan • *Instagram*: norahgn

Karen Clements of Knit 1 LA is a knit and crochet pattern designer specializing in heavier gauge yarns. Growing up in a family of knitters and sewers has fostered a lifelong enthusiasm for fiber that she loves to share, especially with her two young daughters. You can find her patterns on her website, at Ravelry, and on Etsy.

Ravelry: designers/Karen-Clements • *Instagram*: knit1LA •
• *Etsy*: Etsy.com/shop/karenclements

Vicki Stiefel's fantasy-suspense series launched with *Chest of Bone*, the tale of a Mage, a Monster, and a Mission. Her mystery/thrillers include *Body Parts, The Dead Stone, The Grief Shop,* and *The Bone Man*. She co-wrote (with Lisa Souza) *10 Secrets of the LaidBack Knitters*. Vicki taught fiction writing and modern media at Clark University. She mentors writers and students, and critiques writing in a variety of genres. She adores her family and is passionate about scuba diving and fly fishing and knitting, as well as musical comedy scores, which she sings in the shower. The Afterworld Chronicles' second novel, *Chest of Stone*, will hit shelves Nov. 2017, and she is pounding the keys on the series' third novel, *Chest of Air*. Visit with her at:

www.VickiStiefel.com • *Facebook*: vickistiefelauthor, vicki.stiefel.5
• *Instagram*: vickistiefel • *Ravelry*: people/VickiStiefel

Clea's Vest by Karen Clements

Materials:

Yarn: Cadena I by Illimani
49 yards/45 meters 100 gr
4 skeins
Needles: US 17/15mm
24" circular
Darning Needle, Stitch Markers

Gauge:

Brioche Rib:
Multiple of 2
Row 1: Sl 1, K to end
Row 2: Sl 1, *K1, K1b*, K3
Repeat Row 2 only
7 sts x 16 rows = 4"/10cm

Glossary:

K: knit
K1b: knit into the center of the knit stitch in the row below letting the knit stitch that is on the needle drop off to "rest" on the stitch just knit.
Garter Stitch: Knit every row.
RS: right side
WS: wrong side
Sts: stitches
Sl 1: Slip 1 stitch from left needle purlwise.
PU: pick up
*: repeat
BO: bind or cast off

Clea Reese is an FBI interrogation specialist on forced leave, a skilled mentalist, and an empath. Fierce, yet kind, she knits as she interrogates, drawing secrets from the guilty as she pulls yarn from tvhe skein. Unbeknownst to her, she is also a powerful, unawakened Mage, as well as half Fae, and the singular Key to the Chest of Bone. When her mentor is killed, she vows revenge, a path that can lead to her salvation or her destruction. Of course she dons Karen's cozy vest for her hunt.

"Acknowledge and accept, Clea. You are the magic."
~ Dave Cochran, *Chest of Bone*

Designer Notes:

This vest is worked in one piece starting with the bottom of the back. At the shoulders the stitches are separated into 2 sections to create the front. Side seams are sewn after the bottom band of Garter Stitch is worked. And lastly, a collar is added by picking up stitches along the front opening and worked as the bottom band in Garter Stitch.

The Brioche Rib creates a dense fabric with some elasticity as seen in the gauge photos on page 4.

If making any adjustments to the length of the vest always make the front 3″ shorter than the back. Making adjustments to the length of the piece will require more yarn.

START
Using a Provisional Cast On, cast on 28 (32, 36, 40) sts.
Row 1: Sl 1, K to end.
Row 2: Work Row 2 of Brioche Rib for 14" (14.25", 14.5", 14.75").

Divide for the Front
The front is worked simultaneously with 2 balls of yarn, one ball for each side.
Row 1: Sl 1, work Row 2 of Brioche Rib over the next 10 (12, 14, 16) sts, K3. Stop here and with a 2nd ball of yarn work the remaining sts as: Sl 1, work Row 2 of Brioche Rib over the next 13 (15, 17, 19) sts.
Continue to slip the first stitch of every row on BOTH of the front pieces. Work Row 2 of Brioche Rib for 11" (11.25", 11.5", 11.75").
Front & Back completed, ready for bottom border.
Back panel should be 3"/7.5cm longer than front.

Bottom Border
Beginning on the RS and the Left Front, place all the stitches from the Left Front, Back and Right Front onto the needle (see photo p7 for reference).
Continue slipping the 1st stitch of each row and Knit 5 rows.
Bind off.
Sew the side seams for at least 4" or until desired depth.

Armholes Working from the RS and starting at the bottom of the armhole, *pick up a stitch along the armhole opening edge and immediately bind off the stitch*, repeat from * to * until all armhole stitches have been worked.

Collar
With RS facing, pick up stitches along the front openings. At the bottom of the U shape pick up 4 stitches placing a marker on both sides of these 4 stitches (see photo on page 4). Increases will be made on both sides of the markers.

Row 1: Sl 1, K to 1 stitch before the marker, kfb, sl m, kfb, k to 1st before the 2nd marker, kfb, sl m, kfb, k to end.
Rows 2 & 3: Sl 1, K to end.
Row 4: Repeat Row 1.
BO. Weave in all ends.

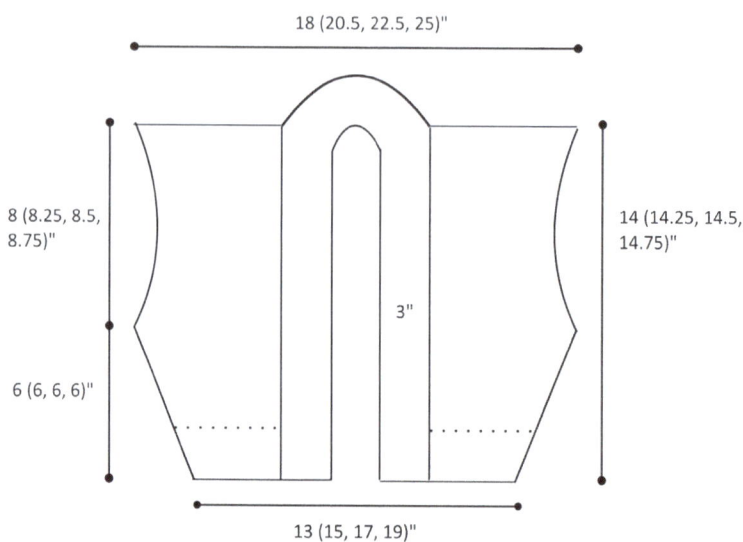

18 (20.5, 22.5, 25)"

8 (8.25, 8.5, 8.75)"

14 (14.25, 14.5, 14.75)"

3"

6 (6, 6, 6)"

13 (15, 17, 19)"

A note on blocking:

After trying on the vest I decided to do a light steaming with my iron instead of a wet block in order to set the stitches. The measurements in the schematic below were taken after steam blocking.

When I was blocking I didn't pull on the vest to open the stitches up, if anything I pushed them in slightly. It is important to note that as you wear the vest the stitch pattern does open up or widen somewhat so there is a bit of latitude in regards to the schematic.

Also, since the Brioche Rib has some elasticity there is leeway if you would like to open the stitches a little by pulling on the piece. If you do so realize the measurements on the schematic will not match the piece you are blocking but again, should be used simply as a guide.

This shows the stitch pattern pushed in. Notice how there are 4 vertical columns of the K stitch within the 4 inches of the tape measure

This shows the stitch pattern pulled slightly. Notice how there are now 3 vertical columns of the K stitch within the 4 inches of the tape measure

The front folded over the back. If adjusting the length, make the front 3" shorter than the back.

Markers showing the center 4 stitches of the picked up collar stitches.

The front and back on one needle, ready to start the bottom border.

A Very Special Project by Vicki Stiefel

A Short Story of the Afterworld Chronicles

Clea Reese awakened with the suddenness of ice on flesh. She jerked up, hands scrabbling across the sheets. The room was freezing. The comforter lay on the floor in a heap and she was coated in sweat. Her hands shook as she raked them through her hair once, twice.

Her dream couldn't have been real. But it had been so vivid her tongue still tasted the chocolate ice cream she'd eaten in her treehouse. She shook her head. Made no sense.

Orphaned at three-years-old, she couldn't picture her mam or her da. She had no photos of them, no mementos, nothing. Yet she'd seen them, crystal, last night while sleeping.

She dragged the comforter off the floor and wrapped it around her shivering body. She had to understand. She closed her eyes and allowed the dream to reform.

Da was knitting. Maybe he was making something for her birthday! In two days, she'd be a big girl of four.

She kept still as the pretty carving Da kept on his desk, but with her eyes she followed Da's needles as they moved smooth and steady. They hummed a rhythm inside her. Finally, she couldn't stand it, so on tiptoe she walked toward the big red chair where Da sat, her eyes glued to his knitting. So many different strands twisted together to form the pattern's colors. Like a sunset—peach and orange and lemon. Beautiful.

More than anything, she wanted to learn to knit just like her da. But there was a problem…

She drew close. "Is today the day, Da?" she whispered in his ear. She made her voice bright and pretty so he would say yes.

His glasses slid down his nose, like always. His smile confused her, for it was both warm and sad. "I'm afraid not, little Clea."

Her fist's clenched. She wouldn't have a tantrum. Da hated those. But her blood bubbled, because she wanted this *so much*. She threw out her chubby arms, wiggled her stubby fingers. "Why, Da? Why not today?"

"Soon, baby girl. Soon. But not today."

The next day, she pulled on her overall jeans and buttoned up her favorite flower shirt with ruffles. She went to show Mam and Da what she'd picked out, but when she got to their door, they we're arguing, always arguing. She peeked through the crack in the door.

"She is too young to knit!" her mam said.

"She is exceptional," Da said. "She deserves to try."

"Not today!"

"These are perilous times, my love. The earlier she learns, the safer she will be."

"No." Mam tapped her foot. "To placate the little beast, I got her a kitten."

"A *what*?"

"A calico kitten. I found it in the wood."

Da's face got all red. "You went to the wood alone? Why? It's dangerous, deadly."

Her mam did that slow laugh that Clea didn't like. "Not to me."

When her da's footsteps neared the door, she scampered away. His face was hard and mean looking when he stormed out, his fingers curled into fists. He sat on the couch, face so tight, and he punched a pillow. Then he leaned his elbows on his knees and covered his face with his hands.

Clea sat on the floor of her room on the pretty rug with pink roses. It was soft, and the kitty would like that. She was trying to pick a name. Kitty was tiny, with black eyes and white and black and orange fur. She almost fit in Clea's palm.

Names were hard. Da said they were important. "Should I call you Meow?"

The kitty spat at her.

That wasn't good. She smiled. "Fluffy?"

The kitty hissed.

Oh, no. Maybe… "Pansy."

The kitty pounced on Clea's chest, stretched her neck, and let out a fierce growl that was very un-kitty like.

"How am I supposed to name you if you don't like any of the names I pick?"

The kitty leapt off her and pranced over to the shelf that held all Clea's favorite books. She batted her paw against one book, a big fat red one. Clea ran over, terrified. If kitty scratched the book, Clea'd be in big trouble. Mam would yell and storm about and tell her that she was going to declaw that mean kitty. It wasn't Clea's fault that the kitty didn't like her mam.

But the book was fine. Clea sighed with relief. The book was her second favorite, and even though she'd only just begun to read, she knew this book's title by heart. Stitch guide. So many pretty pictures of different kinds curls and twists, just like Da knit. All the stitches were in different colors, too, and she loved the way they wove into patterns, like arrows and stars and bumpy streams that Da called cables.

She raced over to the kitty. "You want me to call you Stitch?"

The kitty snarled and spit at her.

"You want me to call you Book?"

Kitty's eyes glowed a bright gold.

She sat hard on her bum. That was scary, but kitty's eyes were green again. Had she really seen that? Da always said she had a big imagination. Except she *had* seen it.

So why couldn't she think up a name that kitty liked? She had to have a name!

She'd go ask Da.

She searched, and she ended up in the study. He did a lot of studying. She found him bent over a big fat book, his pretty blonde hair tied back. She thought he should wear a pink ribbon to tie his hair. He said boys didn't usually wear pink. The lamplight glinted on his gold earring.

"Da? When can I have a gold earring in my ear?"

He swiveled in his chair to face her, his smile bright. Her heart got all happy. "Someday, but not for a long time, pumpkin."

She forgot why she went looking for Da, so she asked instead, "Is Mam home?"

"No."

"Where is she?"

He frowned. "She's gone to the wood."

"I like the wood, Da, but sometimes it's dark and scary and mean."

"Come here, pumpkin." He held out his arms and lifted Clea into his lap. She settled, so warm and cozy.

Kitty meowed, and she remembered why she was here! "I need to find a name for my kitty!"

"We can work on that." He rose from his chair and, carrying her, he walked to the study door, closed it, and turned the lock.

Once they were settled again in his chair, he leaned close and said, "We can work on kitty's name or I can teach you to knit."

Clea clapped. "Knit! Knit! Knit!"

Many weeks later, she was in her room, working on her knitting. She was proud. So proud. Da said she was a good knitter. Very, very good. He said today he had a surprise for her. She knew it had to be about her knitting, which was a secret from Mam, so she practiced very hard. Whenever she practiced kitty was there. She was a nosy kitty.

Kitty would bat at the yarn when Clea was trying so hard to make a stitch. She ignored her. Sometimes, kitty hid in her yarn bag. And sometimes, when she missed a stitch, kitty would bite her.

Kitty still didn't have a name. Fussy, that's what Da said. But kitty didn't like the name Fussy, either. Mam didn't understand why it was so hard to name her kitty. Neither Da, nor she ever told Mam about the hissing and spitting and biting. Mam wouldn't understand, and she'd get mad. She wouldn't understand about her knitting, either. That would make her mad, too. But she was dying to show Mam.

So today she practiced because something exciting was going to happen. She had learned the knit stitch and the purl stitch. The garter, which was easy, and the stockinette, which she couldn't pronounce. The seed stitch, which was pretty, but it was also annoying, and the purl ridge, which was fun. Bamboo and basket weave, too, and Da had made her memorize all of them. She had. Last week, she practiced the arrow stitch and feather and fan. They all were mostly fun, except for that seed stitch. Da said she was exceptional and especially adept at her craft. She didn't know exactly what that meant. Whatever he showed her today, she would make him glad he was teaching her.

Da's footfalls sounded on the stairs, and she got all tingly with excitement. Kitty meowed, and stood, arching her back. When Da walked in he closed the door behind him and sat across from her on the floor.

"See?" She held the scarf she was knitting with the tiles stitch. A blue scarf the color of a lake and Da's eyes.

"Beautiful, pumpkin. You're awfully good." He smoothed over her hair. "I think you're ready to try."

"Try what, Da?"

He grinned, shook his head. "You'll see." He rubbed his earring.

That told her he was excited, too. "A new stitch?"

"No. Put your knitting in its bag."

That didn't make any sense, but she did as asked, giving the soft wool one final rub before putting it away.

"Now raise your hands," he said. "Palms out. Good. Now we are going to play a pretend game."

She loved pretend games!

"Imagine your knitting in front of you and you're going to knit the garter stitch."

Easy peasy. She did as he asked, even if it felt silly.

"Remember that movie we loved, *Star Wars*? Remember what a bold Jedi Luke was?"

She giggled. "I do."

"You don't have a light saber, but you do have your knitting. So I want you to be bold, like a Jedi, and knit that stitch again!"

Da's voice changed, like it had more layers, and it boomed, deep and strong. It filled her with bubbles, in her, around her, and she knew exactly what to do.

Her hands flew through the air moving in the pattern she'd practiced so much. And from her palms came streams of light, like fireflies in the summer night. They glowed as they flew from her hands into the air. There, before her, a glowing garter-stitched web formed.

She squealed, and she laughed as she kept the fireflies going and going.

Da laughed, too. A happy sound.

The door crashed open. "What have you done!"

Oh, no! Mam's eyes were black, and she has a frowny face on, the one with all the teeth!

And Clea couldn't control the fireflies, not even a little, and they swarmed around her head.

Heat and pain sizzled through her, and she screamed.

Clea sat on Da's lap in the bathroom, while Mam washed what was left of her hair. All her long pretty curls were gone. Only sticking-up-tufts were left. Mam used soft, gentle strokes, but it still hurt. She would not cry.

She'd disappointed Da. And Mam was mad. She'd disappointed her, too. Mam's face was all tight, her lips a thin line as she rinsed Clea's head and dried it and the tufts with a towel.

Clea looked creepy, like a monster.

She wouldn't cry. She wouldn't.

Except she did, just a little.

"Don't," Mam said, and she put the towel aside, leaned down, and kissed the tears away. "This was my fault, and I'm sorry."

Da's smile began at the corner of his lips.

"I shouldn't have interrupted what you were doing, Clea," Mam said. "Not the way I did. I'm so sorry, little one. I was afraid to lose your babyhood. And once the Magics come…" Mam sighed. "Yet you're obviously ready to learn them. As Da said, you are exceptional."

Da leaned over and kissed Mam, first on her lips, then right on the tip of her pointy ear. He wore a big smile.

"My hair," Clea said. "It's scary." She raised her hand to the few patches left.

"Yes, it is," Mam said in that serious voice of hers. "Now that it's been touched by magic, it will have a mind of its own, I suspect."

"What does that mean?" Clea asked.

"We'll just have to see!" Da said, and he kissed the top of her head.

Clea looked at Mam and bit her lip. "Can I… can I keep knitting? And practicing my fireflies?"

Mam looked at Da, then at Clea.

The door creaked, and kitty pranced into the room and sat at Da's feet.

Mam narrowed her eyes at the kitty, who hissed back at her. Mam lifted a hand to Clea's cheek. "Yes. Your da will teach you to knit and to firefly, as you call it."

Clea clapped. She couldn't stop smiling. And then it came to her. Her kitty's name. She peered down at the her pretty kitty. "What about Firefly?"

Calico kitty Firefly leapt into her lap, gave her a blink with those glowing eyes of amber, and purred.

~The End~

Larrimer's Sweater by Norah Gaughan

Finished measurements
40(44-48-52-56)"chest
26(27-28-29-30)" length

To fit chest 38(42-46-50-54)"
Suggested ease: Positive 2-4"

Yarn
Harrisville Designs Watershed (100% wool; 110yd / 50 gr skein)
14(16-18-21-23) skeins #969 Granite
1540(1760-1980-2310-2530)yds

Needles
One pair in size US 6
One pair in size US 8
One 16" circular needle (circ) in size US 6

Or size to obtain gauge

Stitch marker(s)
Cable needle

Gauge
17 sts and 28 rows = 4" [10 cm] in st st with larger needles, after blocking
17 sts and 34 rows = 4" [10 cm] in garter stitch with larger needles, after blocking
Cable panel (40sts) = 8" blocked

Stitch patterns
1/1 half twisted rib (even # of sts)
WS *p1, k1tbl, repeat from *, end p1
RS *k1tbl, p1, repeat from *, end k1tbl

James Larrimer is a predator who stalks those who trade in endangered animals. Or so it appears. Originally from Montana, the world is now his hunting ground. While taciturn and deadly, his humor and kindness intrigue Clea. None are prepared for the fusion of Clea's and Larrimer's song, a wild and mysterious resonance which can bind one to the other. He wears several sweaters in the novel. Norah's is his favorite.

Larrimer stepped closer, eyes half-lidded. "Catch more flies with honey."
Clea held her ground. "Careful. Your teeth might rot." ~ Chest of Bone

Cable Panel (over 40 sts) Also shown on chart, see chart for cable definitions
Set up row (WS) – K1, p4, k6, p6, k1, p4, k1, p6, , k6, p4, k1.
1, 5 (RS) – P1, C2R, C2L, p1, k4, p1, k6, p6, k6, p1, k4, p1, C2R, C2L, p1
2, 6 (WS) – K1, p4, (k6, p6) twice, k6, p4, k1.
3 (RS) – P1, C2L, C2R, p1, k4, p1, C6R, p1, k4, p1, C6L, p1, k4, p1, C2L, C2R, p1
4 (WS) – K1, p4, k6, p6, k1, p4, k1, p6, k6, p4, k1
7 (RS) – P1, C2L, C2R, p1, k4, p1, k6, p1, k4, p1, k6, p1, k4, p1, C2L, C2R, p1
8 (WS) – K1, p4, k6, p6, k1, p4, k1, p6, k6, p4, k1
Repeat rows 1-8

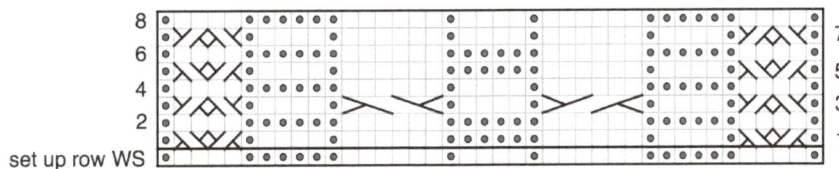

40 sts

KEY

⊡ purl on RS, knit on WS

☐ knit on RS, purl on WS

⅄⅄ C2R 1 on CN in back, k1, k1 from CN

ⅩⅩ C2L 1 on CN in front, k1, k1 from CN

⟩⟨ C6R 3 on CN in back, k3, k3 from CN

⟩⟨ C6L 3 on CN in front, K3, k3 from CN

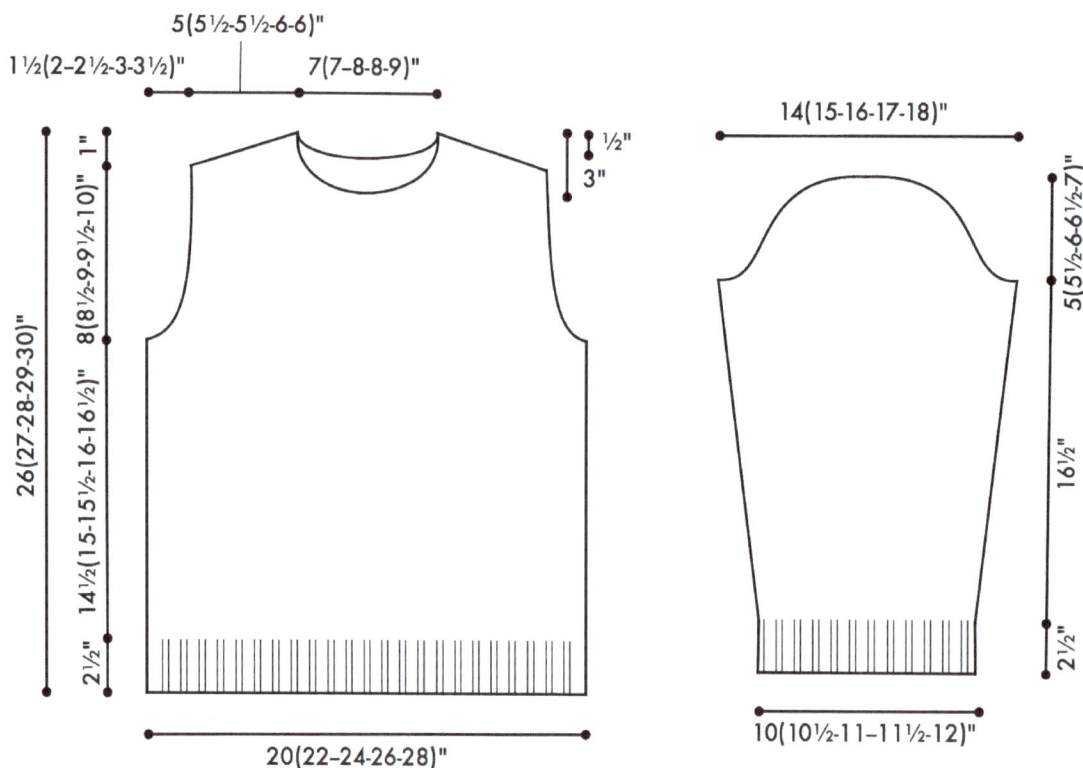

Alternating cable cast on

Put a slip knot on your LH needle. Knit into it, pull up loop and place on the needle. Now purl one on by putting your RH needle between the first 2 sts FROM THE BACK purling, and placing that loop on the needle. Then knit one on by putting your RH needle between the last 2 sts FROM THE FRONT, knitting and placing that loop on the needle. Alternate purling one on and knitting one on.

Hint: If you aren't sure which st to do next – the yarn is alway where you don't want it. If you need to K next your yarn will be in the front and you need to bring it to the back, etc. Looking at the cast on the sts that seem to sink in will be purls and the ones that stand out will be knits. Your first stitch should be a knit, but double check by looking a few sts in and counting back to the tip.

Back

With smaller needles cast on 98(106-116-122-132) sts using the alternating cable cast-on. Work in 1/1 half twisted rib for 2½", ending with a WS row. Change to larger needles and knit one row increasing 0(0-1-0-1)st –98(106-115-122-131) sts

Set up patterns (WS row) – Knit 6(9-12-14-17) work set up row of chart, knit 6(8-11-14-17), work set up row of chart, knit 6(9-12-14-17)
Then, work all rows (before shaping) – Knit 6(9-12-14-17), work next row of chart, knit 6(8-11-14-17), work next row of chart, knit 6(9-12-14-17).
Work straight until piece measures 17(17½-18-18½-19)" from the beginning.

Shape armholes - Keeping in pattern as established, bind off 3 sts at the beg of the next 2 rows. Bind off 2 sts at the beg of the next 2(2-4-6-6) rows. Next row, dec row (RS)– K1, k2tog, work to last 3 sts, ssk, k1. Repeat dec row every RS row 0(2-3-3-5) times more – 86(90-93-96-101) sts. Work straight in patterns established until piece measures 8(8½-9-9½-10)" from the beg of armhole, ending with a WS row.

Shape shoulders and back neck at the same time - Bind off 5(5-5-5-6) sts at the beg of the next 4 rows – 66(70-73-76-77) sts remain. Mark center 22(24-27-30-31) sts. Bind off 5(6-6-6-6) sts, work to marker. Join new yarn, bind off center sts and work to end of row. Turn, bind off 5(6-6-6-6) sts. Working both sides at once work the neck and shoulder shaping at the same time, by binding off at 5 sts at each neck edge 2 times while binding off 6 sts at each shoulder edge twice more.

Front
Same as back to until piece measures 5(5½-6-6½-7)" from the beg of armhole, ending with a WS row. Shape front neck – mark center 22(24-27-30-33) sts. Work to marker, join new yarn and bind off center sts, work to end of row. Working both sides at once bind off at each neck edge 4 sts once, 3 sts once, 2 sts, one 1 st, once. When piece is same as back to shoulders, bind off at each shoulder 5 sts, 2(1-1-1-0) times, then 6 sts, 2(3-3-3-4) times.

Sleeves
With smaller needles cast on 50(52-54-56-58) sts using the alternating cable cast-on. Work in 1/1 half twisted rib for 2½", ending with a WS row. Change to larger needles and knit one row.

Set up patterns (WS row) – Knit 5(6-7-8-9), work set up row of chart, knit 5(6-7-8-9). Both RS and WS rows – Knit 5(6-7-8-9), work next row of chart, knit 5(6-7-8-9). Work straight for 11 rows, ending with a WS row. Next row inc row – K2, M1, work to last 2 sts, M1, k2. Repeat inc row every 12(12-12-10-10) rows, 7(8-9-10-11) times more – 66(70-74-78-82) sts. Work straight until piece measures 19" from the

beginning, ending with a WS row.

Shape sleeve cap – Bind off 3 sts at the beg of the next 2 rows. Bind off 2 sts at the beg of the next 2 rows. Next row (RS) dec row – k3, k2tog, work to last 5 sts, ssk, k3. Repeat dec row every RS row 4(5-6-6-6) times more, then every 4th row 3(3-4-5-5) times, then every RS row 5(6-6-6-7) times. Bind off 2 sts at the beg of the next 2 rows. Bind off 3 sts at the beg of the next 2 rows. Bind off remaining 20(20-20-22-24) sts.

Finishing

Steam or wet block pieces. Sew shoulder seams. Neck – With smaller needles (circ) and RS facing, starting at the center back neck, pick up 104 (104, 112, 112, 120) sts around neck opening. Work in half twisted 1/1 rib for 3" Break yarn leaving a 24" tail. Fold neckband to inside. Using a tapestry needle, secure stitches to the inside of neck. Sew in sleeves. Sew underarm / side seams.

Bernadette's Shawl by Rosemary (Romi) Hill

Finished Size:
About 72" (183 cm) in width; about 20" (51 cm) in depth.

Materials: Cloudborn Fibers, Highland Worsted (100% fine highland wool; 221 yards (202m)/3.5 oz/100 grams): Stormy Sea, 3 skeins
US 8 (5 mm): 24" or 32" (60 or 80 cm) circular (cir) and 1 double-pointed (dpn) for edging.
stitch markers, tapestry needle, cable needle, blocking wires, t-pins

Gauge (blocked): 13 sts and 28 rows = 4" (10 cm) in garter

Abbreviations
21lpc: place 2 sts on cable needle; hold to front, k1, k2 from cable needle
21rpc: place 1 st on cable needle; hold to back, k2, k1 from cable needle

*Clea's foster mother, **Bernadette,** is seldom without her shawl by Romi. She possesses a passion for Game of Thrones, a sharp tongue, and a hoard of secrets only Clea can unlock.*

"You can have my shotgun," Larrimer said. Bernadette's eyes glowed. "Don't need yours, sonny. Got my own."~ Chest of Bone

BO: bind off
c4b: place 2 sts on cable needle; hold to back, k2, k2 from cable needle
c4f: place 2 sts on cable needle; hold to front, k2, k2 from cable needle
CO: cast on
k: knit
kfb: knit into front and back of 1 st
k2tog: (right leaning decrease) knit 2 stitches together
k2tog tbl: knit 2 stitches together tbl
k tbl: knit through back loop to twist stitch
psso: pass slipped st(s) over
p: purl
pm: place marker
RS: right side
sl m: slip marker
ssk: [slip 1 stitch knitwise] 2 times, slip both stitches back onto left needle, knit stitches together
st(s): stitch(es)
tbl: through back loop
WS: wrong side
wyif: with yarn held to front of work
YO: yarn over

Stretchy bind off

Work 2 sts in pattern, [replace both sts on left needle, k2tog tbl, work 1 st in pattern] to end. Fasten off.

INSTRUCTIONS:

CO 11 sts using knitted cast on.

Row 1: [k1 tbl, kfb] 2 times, pm, k1 tbl 3 times, pm, [kfb, k1 tbl] 2 times: 15 sts

Row 2: k1 tbl, kfb, knit to last 2 sts, kfb, k1 tbl : 17 sts

Row 3: k1 tbl, kfb, knit to 1 stitch before marker, kfb, sl m, k3, sl m, kfb, knit to last 2 sts, kfb, k1 tbl (note: mark RS with a safety pin or waste yarn)

Row 4 and all even numbered rows: k1 tbl, kfb, knit to last 2 sts, kfb, k1 tbl

Work rows 3 and 4 an additional 40 times (each repeat of rows 3 and 4 adds 6 sts). 263 stitches.

Chart Symbols

☐	RS: k; WS: p
—	RS: p; WS: k
Ω	RS: k tbl
Ω	WS: k tbl
☑	sl wyif
⌗	k2tog tbl (1 from edging +1 from shawl body), turn

◺◿	place 2 sts on cable needle; hold to front, k1, k2 from cable needle
◹◿	place 1 st on cable needle; hold to back, k2, k1 from cable needle
◿◺	place 2 sts on cable needle; hold to back, k2, k2 from cable needle
◺◿	place 2 sts on cable needle; hold to front, k2, k2 from cable needle

Edging:

Without breaking working yarn, CO 17 sts using knitted method. Work Edging chart at a 90 degree angle to body of shawl, attaching each right side row to body stitches as follows.

Edging Chart written instructions:

Row 1: k1 tbl 2 times, k14, k2tog tbl (1 from edging +1 from shawl body), turn
Row 2: slip st wyif, k14, k1 tbl 2 times
Row 3: k1 tbl 2 times, k5, c4b, c4f, k1, k2tog tbl (1 from edging +1 from shawl body), turn
Row 4: slip st wyif, k1, p8, k5, k1 tbl 2 times
Row 5: k1 tbl 2 times, k4, 21rpc, k4, 21lpc, k2tog tbl (1 from edging +1 from shawl body), turn
Row 6: slip st wyif, p10, k4, k1 tbl 2 times
Row 7: k1 tbl 2 times, k14, k2tog tbl (1 from edging +1 from shawl body), turn
Row 8: slip st wyif, p10, k4, k1 tbl 2 times

Row 9: k1 tbl 2 times, k4, 21lpc, k4, 21rpc, k2tog tbl (1 from edging +1 from shawl body), turn
Row 10: slip st wyif, k1, p8, k5, k1 tbl 2 times

Row 11: k1 tbl 2 times, k5, c4f, c4b, k1, k2tog tbl (1 from edging +1 from shawl body), turn
Row 12: slip st wyif, k1, p8, k5, k1 tbl 2 times
Row 13: k1 tbl 2 times, k14, k2tog tbl (1 from edging +1 from shawl body), turn
Row 14: slip st wyif, k1, p8, k5, k1 tbl 2 times
Row 15: k1 tbl 2 times, k5, c4b, c4f, k1, k2tog tbl (1 from edging +1 from shawl body), turn
Row 16: slip st wyif, k1, p8, k5, k1 tbl 2 times
Row 17: k1 tbl 2 times, k14, k2tog tbl (1 from edging +1 from shawl body), turn
Row 18: slip st wyif, k1, p8, k5, k1 tbl 2 times
Row 19: k1 tbl 2 times, k5, c4b, c4f, k1, k2tog tbl (1 from edging +1 from shawl body), turn
Row 20: slip st wyif, k1, p8, k5, k1 tbl 2 times
Row 21: k1 tbl 2 times, k4, 21rpc, k4, 21lpc, k2tog tbl (1 from edging +1 from shawl body), turn
Row 22: slip st wyif, p10, k4, k1 tbl 2 times
Row 23: k1 tbl 2 times, k14, k2tog tbl (1 from

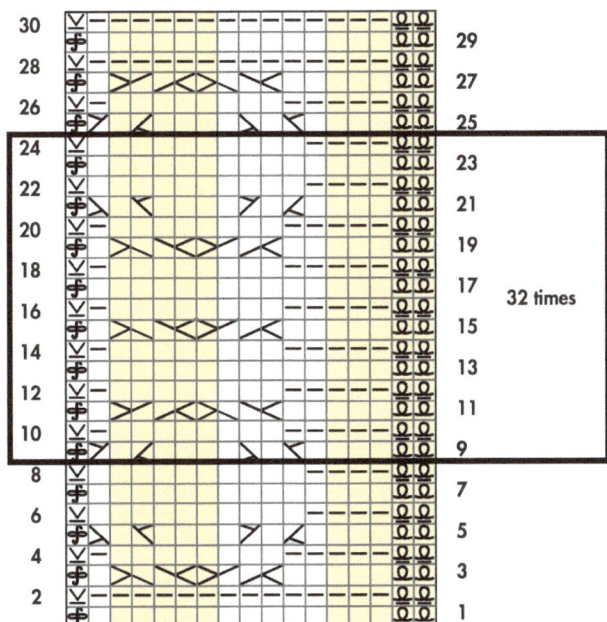

edging chart

Note: Bind off using stretchy bind off on row 30 while working stitches as shown

32 times

edging +1 from shawl body), turn
Row 24: slip st wyif, p10, k4, k1 tbl 2 times

Work rows 9-24 an additional 31 times.

Row 25: k1 tbl 2 times, k4, 21lpc, k4, 21rpc, k2tog tbl (1 from edging +1 from shawl body), turn
Row 26: slip st wyif, k1, p8, k5, k1 tbl 2 times
Row 27: k1 tbl 2 times, k5, c4f, c4b, k1, k2tog tbl (1 from edging +1 from shawl body), turn
Row 28: slip st wyif, k14, k1 tbl 2 times
Row 29: k1 tbl 2 times, k14, k2tog tbl (1 from edging +1 from shawl body), turn
Row 30: slip st wyif, bind off all sts using stretchy bind off. (including slipped stitch)

Finishing:
Wash shawl using wool wash. Weave
blocking wires in and out along top of
shawl, stretch, and pin securely. Weave
blocking wires in and out along bottom
edge, stretch shawl into shape, and
pin securely. Let dry thoroughly before
unpinning. Weave in ends after shawl has
dried.

Mitts for Larrimer by Rosemary (Romi) Hill

Clea knits Larrimer these fingered mitts, by Romi, with their symbolic motif.

"You're still madly inscrutable," Clea said.
Larrimer raised that eyebrow. "Whereas you're simply maddening."

Size: Small {Medium, Large}
Hand Circumference: 7 {8, 9} inches unstretched
Materials: Cloudborn Fibers [100% Fine Highland Wool, 221yds/100g]; Slate Heather; 1 skein

1 - each set US 5/3.75mm and US 6/4mm double pointed needles OR 2 - sets each US 5/3.75mm and US 6/4mm circular needles
waste yarn, stitch markers, tapestry needle, cable needle
spare circular needle, US 3 or smaller, to hold stitches

Gauge (unblocked): 18 sts/24 rows = 4"/10cm in stockinette stitch using larger needles
Every knitter's gauge is different; please check gauge!

Stitches used:
Reverse stockinette stitch: with RS facing, purl every row
Stockinette stitch: with RS facing, knit every row

Abbreviations:
BO: bind off
c6l (cable 6 stitches left): slip 3 sts onto cable needle and hold to front; k3, k3 from cable needle
c6r (cable 6 stitches right): slip 3 sts onto cable needle and hold to back; k3, k3 from cable needle

CO: cast on
k: knit
k2tog tbl: (left leaning decrease) knit 2 stitches together tbl
k tbl: knit through back loop to twist stitch
M1: make knit stitch by pulling up bar between sts, twisting and knitting into loop
M1L: make knit stitch by pulling up bar between sts, twisting bar to the left, and knitting into loop
M1R: make knit stitch by pulling up bar between sts, twisting bar to right, and knitting into loop
p2tog: purl 2 sts together
pm: place marker
p: purl
RS: right side
sl m: slip marker
st(s): stitch(es)
WS: wrong side

Note: instructions are given for both mitts where possible. Where mitts differ, separate instructions are given for left and right mitts.

LEFT AND RIGHT MITTS
Cast on and ribbing:

CO 34 {40, 44} sts using smaller needles.

Arrange sts evenly on 4 double pointed needles or on two circular needles. Place marker and join to work in the round, being careful not to twist cast on round.

Work 3 rounds of reverse stockinette stitch, then work in k1 tbl, p1 ribbing for 2 {2.5, 3} inches.

Switch to larger needles.

Right Mitt ONLY:
Change to working in stockinette stitch with cable pattern, as follows.
Rounds 1 and 2: knit
Round 3: knit 2 {4, 5} sts, c6l, c6r, knit to end.
Rounds 4-8: knit

Round 9: knit 2 {4, 5} sts, c6l, c6r, knit 3 {4, 5} sts, pm, M1, pm, knit to end.
Round 10: knit
Round 11: knit to marker, sl m, M1L, k1, M1R, sl m, knit to end
Round 12: knit
Round 13: knit to marker, sl m, M1L, k3, M1R, sl m, knit to end: 5 sts in thumb gusset
Round 14: knit

Round 15: knit 2 {4, 5} sts, c6l, c6r, knit 3 {4, 5} sts, sl m, M1L, knit to marker, M1R, sl m, knit to end.
Round 16: knit
Round 17: knit to marker, sl m, M1L, knit to marker, M1R, sl m, knit to end
Round 18: knit
Rounds 19 and 20: repeat rounds 17 and 18: 11 sts in thumb gusset

Small ONLY: Repeat rounds 15 and 16: 13 sts in thumb gusset
Work 4 rounds in stockinette stitch
Divide thumb sts: k2 sts, c6l, c6r, k3, remove marker, place 13 gusset sts on waste yarn, remove marker, CO 1 st over gap, knit to end: 35 working sts

Medium ONLY: Repeat rounds 15-18: 15 sts in thumb gusset
Work 2 rounds in stockinette stitch.
Next round: k4, c6l, c6r, knit to end.
Work 3 rounds in stockinette stitch.
Divide thumb sts: knit to marker, remove marker, place 15 gusset sts on waste yarn, remove marker, CO 1 st over gap, knit to end: 41 working sts
Work 1 round in stockinette stitch.
Next round: k4, c6l, c6r, knit to end.

Large ONLY: Repeat rounds 15-20: 17 sts in thumb gusset
Next round: k5, c6l, c6r, knit to end.
Work 5 rounds in stockinette stitch.
Next round: k5, c6l, c6r, knit to end.
Work one round in stockinette stitch.
Divide thumb sts: knit to marker, remove marker, place 17 gusset sts on waste yarn, remove marker, CO 1 st over gap, knit to end: 45 working sts

Left Mitt ONLY:
Change to working in stockinette stitch with cable pattern, as follows.
Rounds 1 and 2: knit
Round 3: knit 20 {24, 27} sts, c6l, c6r, knit to end.
Rounds 4-8: knit

Round 9: knit 17 {20, 22} sts, pm, M1, pm, knit 3 {4, 5} sts, c6l, c6r, knit to end.
Round 10: knit
Round 11: knit to marker, sl m, M1L, k1, M1R, sl m, knit to end
Round 12: knit
Round 13: knit to marker, sl m, M1L, k3, M1R, sl m, knit to end: 5 sts in thumb gusset
Round 14: knit

Round 15: knit 17 {20, 22} sts, sl m, M1L, knit to marker, M1R, sl m, knit 3 {4, 5} sts, c6l, c6r, knit to end.
Round 16: knit
Round 17: knit to marker, sl m, M1L, knit to marker, M1R, sl m, knit to end
Round 18: knit
Rounds 19 and 20: repeat rounds 17 and 18: 11 sts in thumb gusset

Small ONLY: Repeat rounds 15 and 16: 13 sts in thumb gusset
Work four rounds in stockinette stitch
Divide thumb sts: knit to marker, remove marker, place 13 gusset sts on waste yarn, remove marker, CO 1 st over gap, k3, c6l, c6r, knit to end: 35 working sts

Medium ONLY: Repeat rounds 15-18: 15 sts in thumb gusset
Work 2 rounds in stockinette stitch
Next round: [knit to marker, sl m] 2 times, k4, c6l, c6r, knit to end.
Work 3 rounds in stockinette stitch.
Divide thumb sts: knit to marker, remove marker, place 15 gusset sts on waste yarn, CO 1 st over gap, sl m, knit to end: 41 working sts
Work 1 round in stockinette stitch.
Next round: knit to marker, remove marker, k4, c6l, c6r, knit to end.

Large ONLY: Repeat rounds 15-20: 17 sts in thumb gusset
Next round: [knit to marker, sl m] 2 times, k5, c6l, c6r, knit to end.
Work 5 rounds in stockinette stitch.
Next round: [knit to marker, sl m] 2 times, k5, c6l, c6r, knit to end.
Work one round in stockinette stitch.
Divide thumb sts: knit to marker, remove marker, place 17 gusset sts on waste yarn, remove marker, CO 1 st over gap, knit to end: 45 working sts

LEFT AND RIGHT MITTS
All sizes: work 5 rounds in stockinette stitch.
Switch to smaller needles and work in stockinette stitch until mitt measures 1 {1-1/2, 2} inches above separation for thumb.

Little Finger:
Knit 4 {5, 6} sts, and put 28 {32, 34} sts on spare circular needle. CO 1 st over gap and knit to end: 8 {10, 12} working sts. Work in k1 tbl, p1 ribbing for 1/2 {3/4, 1} inch(es) using dpns or 2 circular needles. Bind off loosely in pattern.

Upper Hand:
Place held sts on working needles. Join yarn, pick up and knit 2 sts along CO edge at base of little finger. Work stockinette stitch in the round for 1/4 {1/4, 1/2} inches: 30 {34, 36} sts

Ring Finger:
Knit 5 {6, 6} sts and place 20 {22, 24} sts on spare circular needle. CO 1 {1, 2} sts over gap and

knit 5 {6, 6} sts: 11 {13, 14} sts.

Small and medium ONLY: [k1 tbl, p1] 2 times, k1 tbl, p2tog, and work [k1 tbl, p1] to end.

ALL SIZES: work in k1 tbl, p1 ribbing for a total of 3/4 {1, 1-1/4} inch(es) using dpns or 2 circular needles. Bind off loosely in pattern.

Middle Finger:
Rejoin yarn; pick up and knit 2 sts at base of ring finger. Knit first 5 {5, 6} held sts onto working needles. CO 1 {2, 2} sts over gap, place last 5 {5, 6} held sts (from other end of spare circular needle) on working needles and knit sts: 13 {14, 16} working sts.

Small ONLY: [k1 tbl, p1] 3 times, k2tog tbl, p1, and work [k1 tbl, p1] to end.

ALL SIZES: work in k1 tbl, p1 ribbing for a total of 3/4 {1, 1-1/4} inch(es) using dpns or 2 circular needles. Bind off loosely in pattern.

Index Finger:
Place remaining sts on working needles. Rejoin yarn; pick up and knit 2 {2, 4} at base of middle finger: 12 {14, 16} working sts. Work in k1 tbl, p1 ribbing for a total of 3/4 {1, 1-1/4} inch(es) using dpns or 2 circular needles. Bind off loosely in pattern.

Thumb:
Place thumb gusset sts on working needles, join yarn and pick up and knit 1 sts over gap between hand and thumb: 14 {16, 18} sts. Work in k1 tbl, p1 ribbing for a total of 3/4 {1, 1-1/4} inch(es) using dpns or 2 circular needles. Bind off loosely in pattern.

Finishing:
Sew in ends, closing up holes between fingers and thumb, and hand. Wash using wool wash. Remove excess water and lay flat to block. When thoroughly dry, wear and enjoy!

Lulu's Mitts by Rosemary (Romi) Hill

Fifteen-year-old **Lulu Cochran's** strength comes from the deep and abiding love of her father and her innate will to survive. When deadly events destroy her stable world, Lulu's is orphaned and flung into a chaos of uncertainty. Will she take the right path or race to her doom? Clea loves Lulu, and she pours that love into each stitch she knits.

"Lulu bobbed up from behind the counter, eyes bright as amethysts, hair a blaze of copper, wearing a baggy black NYU sweatshirt. An immense gun quivered in her outstretched hands." ~ Chest of Bone

Size: Small {Medium, Large}
Hand Circumference: 7 {8, 9} inches unstretched

Materials: Cloudborn Fibers [100% Fine Highland Wool, 221yds/100g]; Maize Heather; 1 skein

1 - each set US 5/3.75mm and US 6/4mm double pointed needles OR 2 - sets each US 5/3.75mm and US 6/4mm circular needles
waste yarn, stitch markers, tapestry needle, cable needle spare circular needle, US 3 or smaller, to hold stitches

Gauge (unblocked): 18 sts/24 rows = 4"/10cm in stockinette stitch using larger needles
Every knitter's gauge is different; please check gauge!

Stitches used:
Reverse stockinette stitch: with RS facing, purl every row
Stockinette stitch: with RS facing, knit every row

Abbreviations:

BO: bind off

c6l (cable 6 stitches left): slip 3 sts onto cable needle and hold to front; k3, k3 from cable needle

c6r (cable 6 stitches right): slip 3 sts onto cable needle and hold to back; k3, k3 from cable needle

CO: cast on

k: knit

k2tog tbl: (left leaning decrease) knit 2 stitches together tbl

k tbl: knit through back loop to twist stitch

M1: make knit stitch by pulling up bar between sts, twisting and knitting into loop

M1L: make knit stitch by pulling up bar between sts, twisting bar to the left, and knitting into loop

M1R: make knit stitch by pulling up bar between sts, twisting bar to right, and knitting into loop

p2tog: purl 2 sts together

pm: place marker

p: purl

RS: right side

sl m: slip marker

st(s): stitch(es)

WS: wrong side

Note: instructions are given for both mitts where possible. Where mitts differ, separate instructions are given for left and right mitts.

LEFT AND RIGHT MITTS

Cast on and ribbing:

CO 34 {40, 44} sts using smaller needles.

Arrange sts evenly on 4 double pointed needles or on two circular needles. Place marker and join to work in the round, being careful not to twist cast on round.

Work 3 rounds of reverse stockinette stitch, then work in k1 tbl, p1 ribbing for 2 {2.5, 3} inches.

Switch to larger needles.

Right Mitt ONLY:
Change to working in stockinette stitch with cable pattern, as follows.
Rounds 1 and 2: knit
Round 3: knit 2 {4, 5} sts, c6l, c6r, knit to end.
Rounds 4-8: knit

Round 9: knit 2 {4, 5} sts, c6l, c6r, knit 3 {4, 5} sts, pm, M1, pm, knit to end.
Round 10: knit
Round 11: knit to marker, sl m, M1L, k1, M1R, sl m, knit to end
Round 12: knit
Round 13: knit to marker, sl m, M1L, k3, M1R, sl m, knit to end: 5 sts in thumb gusset
Round 14: knit

Round 15: knit 2 {4, 5} sts, c6l, c6r, knit 3 {4, 5} sts, sl m, M1L, knit to marker, M1R, sl m, knit to end.
Round 16: knit
Round 17: knit to marker, sl m, M1L, knit to marker, M1R, sl m, knit to end
Round 18: knit
Rounds 19 and 20: repeat rounds 17 and 18: 11 sts in thumb gusset

Small ONLY: Repeat rounds 15 and 16: 13 sts in thumb gusset
Work 4 rounds in stockinette stitch
Divide thumb sts: k2 sts, c6l, c6r, k3, remove marker, place 13 gusset sts on waste yarn, remove marker, CO 1 st over gap, knit to end: 35 working sts

Medium ONLY: Repeat rounds 15-18: 15 sts in thumb gusset
Work 2 rounds in stockinette stitch.

Next round: k4, c6l, c6r, knit to end.
Work 3 rounds in stockinette stitch.

Divide thumb sts: knit to marker, remove marker, place 15 gusset sts on waste yarn, remove marker, CO 1 st over gap, knit to end: 41 working sts
Work 1 round in stockinette stitch.
Next round: k4, c6l, c6r, knit to end.

Large ONLY: Repeat rounds 15-20: 17 sts in thumb gusset
Next round: k5, c6l, c6r, knit to end.
Work 5 rounds in stockinette stitch.
Next round: k5, c6l, c6r, knit to end.
Work one round in stockinette stitch.
Divide thumb sts: knit to marker, remove marker, place 17 gusset sts on waste yarn, remove marker, CO 1 st over gap, knit to end: 45 working sts

Left Mitt ONLY:
Change to working in stockinette stitch with cable pattern, as follows.
Rounds 1 and 2: knit
Round 3: knit 20 {24, 27} sts, c6l, c6r, knit to end.
Rounds 4-8: knit

Round 9: knit 17 {20, 22} sts, pm, M1, pm, knit 3 {4, 5} sts, c6l, c6r, knit to end.
Round 10: knit
Round 11: knit to marker, sl m, M1L, k1, M1R, sl m, knit to end
Round 12: knit
Round 13: knit to marker, sl m, M1L, k3, M1R, sl m, knit to end: 5 sts in thumb gusset
Round 14: knit
v
Round 15: knit 17 {20, 22} sts, sl m, M1L, knit to marker, M1R, sl m, knit 3 {4, 5} sts, c6l, c6r, knit to end.
Round 16: knit
Round 17: knit to marker, sl m, M1L, knit to marker, M1R, sl m, knit to end
Round 18: knit
Rounds 19 and 20: repeat rounds 17 and 18: 11 sts in thumb gusset

Small ONLY: Repeat rounds 15 and 16: 13 sts in thumb gusset
Work four rounds in stockinette stitch
Divide thumb sts: knit to marker, remove marker, place 13 gusset sts on waste yarn, remove marker, CO 1 st over gap, k3, c6l, c6r, knit to end: 35 working sts

Medium ONLY: Repeat rounds 15-18: 15 sts in thumb gusset
Work 2 rounds in stockinette stitch

Next round: [knit to marker, sl m] 2 times, k4, c6l, c6r, knit to end.
Work 3 rounds in stockinette stitch.
Divide thumb sts: knit to marker, remove marker, place 15 gusset sts on waste yarn, CO 1 st over gap, sl m, knit to end: 41 working sts
Work 1 round in stockinette stitch.
Next round: knit to marker, remove marker, k4, c6l, c6r, knit to end.

Large ONLY: Repeat rounds 15-20: 17 sts in thumb gusset
Next round: [knit to marker, sl m] 2 times, k5, c6l, c6r, knit to end.
Work 5 rounds in stockinette stitch.
Next round: [knit to marker, sl m] 2 times, k5, c6l, c6r, knit to end.
Work one round in stockinette stitch.
Divide thumb sts: knit to marker, remove marker, place 17 gusset sts on waste yarn, remove marker, CO 1 st over gap, knit to end: 45 working sts

LEFT AND RIGHT MITTS
All sizes: work 5 rounds in stockinette stitch.
Switch to smaller needles and work in stockinette stitch until mitt measures 1 {1-1/2, 2} inches above separation for thumb.

ALL SIZES
Next round: [k1 tbl, p1] to 3 sts before end of round, k1 tbl, p2tog.
Work in k1 tbl, p1 ribbing for a total of 3/4 {1, 1-1/4} inch(es) (including first round of ribbing) using dpns or 2 circular needles. Bind off loosely in pattern.

Thumb:
Place thumb gusset sts on working needles, join yarn and pick up and knit 1 sts over gap between hand and thumb: 14 {16, 18} sts. Work in k1 tbl, p1 ribbing for a total of 3/4 {1, 1-1/4} inch(es) using dpns or 2 circular needles. Bind off loosely in pattern.

Finishing:
Sew in ends, closing up holes between hand and thumb. Wash using wool wash. Remove excess water and lay flat to block. When thoroughly dry, wear and enjoy!

Chest of Bone (C1&2) by Vicki Stiefel

Venecia Herkimer Dragon

CHAPTER 1

The word "former" sucks. Former friend. Former lover. Former astronaut. Former anything implies that the past was better than the now.

I don't believe that. All you have is now, and maybe a few tomorrows… if you're lucky.

Destined for the Feed and Seed, I turned from pondering "big thoughts" and flicked on my audiobook as my Tahoe sped down Route 202 in Midborough. Stark and lonely in its winter cloak, the road was lined with snow-dusted pines, frozen marsh, and the occasional house. As I crested the rise of the small hill, something down below prowled onto the pavement. And sat. In the middle of the road. I pressed the brake on the downslope, slowed the truck.

I squinted into the bright morning sun. What the hell?

A huge black cat sat smack on the double yellow line where the road leveled off. Black cats were bad luck.

And this black cat was the size of a Harley. It was beyond bad luck. It was scary as shit. It also made me question my sanity.

I'd been doing that a lot lately, the sanity thing.

I braked.

From twenty feet away, the cat lunged, a blur, landing inches from my bumper.

I jerked the wheel, careened off the road toward the snowy pines to avoid hitting the humongous black panther that shouldn't exist in any reality, no less New Hampshire's. I flung my sanity worries aside. If I crashed into the fast-approaching pine tree, the point would be moot.

Splatting into a tree… I'd never show Dave my pink-tipped blond spikes… never watch his new mentalism effect… never read that book he'd promised me… never again see him. My mentor was "off," something bad going on with him. If the meeting of tree and me happened…

My Tahoe bounced, tipped sideways, and went airborne. The landing thud shook my bones. I slammed the gas, yanked right, avoided an alder stand. And that ginormous pine, looming closer and closer…

I white-knuckled the steering wheel and braced for impact.

Savage anguish lanced through me, a sadist rearranging my atoms. Razors slicing my skin over and over.

No. No. No. Not now… not…

Blind. Blind. Blind. Can't see, can't hear, can't think.

Tried to mantra my way to sanity.

Yeah well, that didn't work.

Being an FBI interrogator sometimes sucked. Being an empath sometimes sucked worse.

Frost iced my skull, my face, my mind, my body.

I blacked out.

I awakened. My head rested on my hands, which curled around the steering wheel. I blinked twice. Vision, check. Fingers and toes, check. Torso and legs, check. Brain, whatever.

The world refocused, a lens iris expanding. The truck sat in the middle of a frozen marsh, banded on three sides by pine, spruce, and birch. I was uninjured, the truck—pristine.

I turned the ignition, and the Tahoe purred to life.

Fucking A. What the hell had just…

Screw it. I was alive. The truck was functional.

My phone read… Damn, Dave's store had been open for an hour. I was late.

The day had grown cloudy by the time I pulled into the Midborough Feed and Seed. In the ashen light, shadows of marsh, meadow, and pine surrounded the large blue building shaped like a U, its "Blue Seal" banner snapping in the wind. No sign of any customers. Bonus. I'd have more time with Dave—mentor, friend, and the only father figure I'd ever known. If anyone could make sense of my latest "adventure," Dave could.

Except a Closed sign hung inside the door. And no twin mutts' noses pressed the glass, awaiting the next arrival.

A terrible wrongness leeched across my skin, coating me like boggy sludge. I jerked the car's door handle.

You're too impulsive. Caution. Always. My foster mother Bernadette's words, carved on my soul.

They'd saved me more than once.

I phoned the store. The machine picked up.

Called Dave's home, hoped he hadn't had to close because of another problem with his teenage daughter, Lulu. No joy on the home machine, either.

I slipped my Glock from its shoulder holster, slid from the truck, and padded to the door. I listened, massaged my clammy skin. Silence. I pushed down the handle—locked—thumbed through my keyring, found the right one, unlocked the door. I eased it open.

Gun in my two-handed grip, barrel pointed dead ahead, I pressed my back to the wall. Inside, that oily wrongness increased. A grim ugliness pervaded the place, tendrils of it, like dirty smoke, seeping from the sales counter that divided the store, maybe thirty feet away. And that smell.

Rotted geraniums and cat urine. Vile. I swallowed, hard.

If anyone hurt Dave, they were toast. I mean, seriously charcoaled briquettes. He was fine, though. Peachy. And worse comes to worst, he knew how to shoot a gun, right? But how well? How good was his aim?

Someone had moved a display, blocking the aisle. I pushed my senses to feel if anyone else was here and caught a faint echo of… pain.

Crouched low, I moved to my left, up an aisle flanked by display shelves. I heard nothing, until…

"Clea."

A ragged whisper. Dave.

I jerked toward the sound, needed to dash. Bernadette's wall of caution slammed into me. I moved silent and smooth down the aisle, toward the counter, toward…

Dave. His back against the counter, legs sprawled. I ran.

Stumbled to a halt, vision blurred. What…? Red? A Rorschach of red. On Dave, the floor, the back of the counter. Legs, torso, arms, face, coated in blood. Shining. Glistening.

I strangled my scream and fell to my knees beside him.

Eyes swollen shut, breathing shallow. Somewhere under all that blood, naked but for a pair of red-soaked boxers…

"Dave," I said, tone hushed.

CHAPTER 2

The man I adored smelled of death. Dozens of cuts slashed his legs, his sleeve-tattooed arms, his torso, his face. His discarded clothes lay in a bloody pile beside him. They must have stripped him before "working" him over. Oh gods. I reached for him, curled my hands. I didn't dare.

"What happened? What can I do?" I fumbled for my phone to call 9-1-1. His bloodied fingers clawed around my wrist.

His eyes slit open, their soft violet capturing me. "No." A whisper.

"But—"

"No." Firmer. Impossible to ignore. Blood trickled from his mouth to his scruff, beaded there.

"The pups?"

"Fine. Locked away." He panted for a moment.

I breathed in a sob, lifted a hand to caress his hair, the one part of him that didn't seem injured. His pain splintered through me. "What hap—"

"No time." He lifted my hand and pressed it to his ruined cheek. "Listen."

"But—"

A faint smile. "Listen, kid." A wheeze. "I'm your guardian. A Guardian."

"Please—"

"Sshhh."

So soft, I strained to hear. I leaned closer.

"I knew you'd come," he said. "I waited. For you. So much still to do. Shield Lulu. Protect you. Take the chest. A… thing… of… power." He grinned then. Always so quick with that grin. "I know, crazy, huh?"

"Yes. Crazy. Whatever you say."

"Damn straight. The panther. She arrived in time."

"She did." How could he know?

And those gentle lips melted into an almost-smile. "Good. Would have taken you. Killed you, too."

"Who, Dave?" My voice hitched. With each of his breaths, viscous blood oozed, stealing his life. "Who did this?"

A long silence, then, "The Storybook. Find it. Green cover you bit. Take it. Read…"

"Dave, who!"

His lips barely moved. I leaned closer.

"Spell. Magic." Dave's grip on my wrist constricted.

Psychic pain crashed over me.

"Tell no one what you hunt."

"I won't."

"Promise." He gritted it out between his teeth.

"I promise." Something shifted inside me.

With his free hand, he cupped my cheek, a tear strolling from his eye. "Love you."

My body shook. "I love you so much." I almost blurted the word "father," for that's what he was to me. Always there. Always present. I couldn't lose him. I couldn't. Live, Dave. Live!

His vise on my right wrist tightened. Electric current zapped up my arm, shocking me.

Pain, so bad my back bowed. As if through a glass, darkly, his sleeve tattoos moved. The Ouroboros morphing into The Dragon sliding into The Eye, then twirling, twirling, a cosmos, a galaxy, a spiral nebula that spun faster and faster, and…

Agony rocked me forward. I screamed, each molecule of my being stung by invisible wasps. Blind. Deaf. Stop. Stop. Stop!

A cooling balm washed over me, like a winter's stream burbling over rocks, soothing my pain, again and again, until it dissolved.

I panted, pressed my free hand to the floor, steadying myself. My head was buried in his shoulder, my body flush against his. Gingerly, I pushed off him and sat back on my heels.

"I've unlocked it." His hand fell away. "Good. Acknowledge and accept. You are the magic."

My breath stuttered, my wrist burned. I rubbed it again and again, as blood seeped through my fingers. Changed.

It was changed.

I was changed.

"Dave?"

His violet eyes dimmed, he panted, thirsty-dog breaths. "I didn't finish. Forgive me."

I cupped his cheeks. "There's nothing to forgive!"

A susurrus of breath. His essence left his body, hovered, then dissipated, raindrops on a lake.

A blink of time. Now, only stillness. Utter. Infinite.

Clues. Of course, I needed to find clues. Who had done this? When? Why?

I scraped a hand through my hair, then stared at my blood-streaked fingers. I shrugged, singularly not giving a shit, then stood and stumbled, breathing deep, sampling the acrid, coppery scent of Dave's blood. It coated my nose, flavored my tongue.

With a mechanical deliberateness, I pulled the nitrile gloves I always carried from my jacket's inner pocket and snapped them on. I walked around the body, feet squishing in the fluids on the linoleum, to the counter. Must find why. Must find them.

I sifted through Feed and Seed papers, some dotted with blood, Dave's blood. Huh. Had to be careful. Preserve the scene. I snorted. That ship had already sailed. The papers—invoices, bills of landing.

Behind the counter, I came up empty, walked toward the office, seeking, hunting, which is when the whining of Dave's dogs from behind the storage room door brought me up short. He must have shut them in when he spotted the men approaching from the parking lot. Which meant he knew or recognized his killers.

Mutt and Jeff assaulted me when I opened the door to the storage room. I grabbed their collars and led them into Dave's office, made sure to close the door, then slipped them biscuits from my pocket. I told the pair to stay. If they found Dave in his condition, they'd go nuts.

The office was trashed. Papers and broken mugs and loose kibbles strewn everywhere. File drawers open, emptied. Pens and ink and chaos. The techs would have a field day.

The techs. I hadn't called it in.

I dialed 9-1-1 and in crisp words, detailed where I was, what I'd found, and barked they should get to Dave's daughter, Lulu, fast.

I wet my lips. Such utter mess!

Maybe he'd hidden something beneath the kneehole of the desk. A clue that would point to his killers or the reasons they'd come a-calling. Yeah, sure, that would make sense.

I got down on hands and knees, face pressed to the desk's edge, and felt beneath its underbelly. I groped. Nothing. Too obvious, for my clever Dave.

My fingers curled into fists, until I felt the bite of my nails, the pain of control.

After three heartbeats, I flexed them, losing balance, slapping them on the floor.

The corner of something hard rested beneath my palm. I wrapped my hand around the edge as I tipped back on my heels to stand.

I held a book. Mylar covered. Old. No jacket, but the blue cloth-covered boards were near perfect and the spine's gilt lettering shined. The original hardcover of *The Once and Future King*, with a red sticky note: For Clea. And then, the joke. Always a terrible joke: What do you call a big pile of kittens? A meowntain.

I almost laughed, except my body began to shake. No. No. No. A tear dripped onto my coat sleeve.

Shit! Dave would kill me if I got tears on the book, he…

No, he wouldn't.

As my tears came faster, my hands reflexively tightened on the book.

The brrring of the landline on the desk froze me.

Get your shit together.

The caller ID read "Lulugirl."

Ring. Ring. Ring.

Soon, Lulugirl. Soon.

I snugged the book inside my leather jacket and left the office.

Back out front, I couldn't look at him. I mean, if I didn't look, he wasn't dead, right? Except the place was so absent of sound. Of life. I allowed my eyes to seek Dave.

So still. So quiet. Dave defined energy, life.

Silence was never so deafening.

I walked over to the remains. The corpse. The non-Dave. Crap, I'd made a mess of the scene. I crouched down. Dave's blood covered me, crusted my face, my boots, my jacket. I scraped my hands across a couple clean spots on my jeans, then reached for my phone, tapped out every word Dave had uttered and emailed the note to myself. Done, I photographed the remains, each slash of cruelty, and took closeups of a couple. How bizarre. Almost as if his skin had split apart from the inside.

And then, I sat on the floor beside my mentor's body, held his stilled hand, and waited for the troops to arrive.

I had no memory of my parents. Not the brush of a hand, a cuddle, a scent. No pictures, no tokens, no tales. Just a void.

A family fostered me until they passed me off to Bernadette and her grandson, Tommy, who was four. So was I, and we were best friends from then on. That was when I met Dave.

He must have been in his twenties when he took me on as a "project." I never knew why. He was a merry man, tall, and sapling thin. His tattoos fascinated me, and he'd laugh, making up stories about each one to entertain a kid starved for affection. He read to me for hours. And I could still feel our quiet joy as we hiked the forests and rock hills of New Hampshire.

I brushed a finger across that hand that had held mine so often.

"You're the world's most stubborn do-gooder." I sniffled. "Study your math. Stand up straight. Yes, you are taking ballet."

We had pure fun when we practiced magic tricks and mentalist reveals.

I squeezed his bloody shoulders. "You brought out the empath in me. Remember how you insisted we first practice on animals? Did I tell you I thought it was really dumb? Pretty sure I did. And people! Oof. Strangers were okay, friends were embarrassing, but the crowds, they were the toughest."

What are they feeling? you'd ask. Are they angry? Sad? Lonely? Joyful?

"You made me open my senses, to feel what others feel, the obvious and the secret. Except, dammit, I feel too much. We weren't done!"

A giggle, then a sob.

"You said it mattered. I should have listened better."

Now what am I supposed to do?

I sat back on my heels and smiled, slow and mean. "I'll catch your killer, Dave. And when I do, I'm gonna skewer him, barbecue him, and feed his entrails to the crows. Yeah, all right, pretty yuck. But I'll get him. First, though, I'm going to go find that kid of yours."

The troops poured in and, per procedure, I was interviewed ad nauseam. I'd put on my FBI persona, which managed to get me through until eyes bored into the back of my skull. I split my focus enough to unfurl my senses. Yeah, a lot of people were surreptitiously watching me, but this was different. One guy's interest was so centered, prickles danced along my skin. As if I were a threat? No, not quite right.

Given my emotionally jagged state, getting a clear read on the watcher was proving problematic. I massaged my still-achy wrist, a physical prompt to aid my concentration, then fine-tuned my senses and lasered my probe.

And gasped, stunned by a mind singular and unique—fierce, calculating, savage in intensity. Other.

Guard. Prey.

A blaze of protectiveness burned me, with low notes of compassion, and higher ones of quarry. Was I the prey?

At which point, a detective's ceaseless questions intruded, going on and on and on. Finally, a state trooper interrupted the man. I pivoted just a hair to eyeball the room.

Gotcha. In a corner perfect for observing the scene, a large man in dark clothes, a shock of raven hair, bronze skinned. If he moved from the shadow, I would see him more clearly. And what was with that strange, almost unnatural vibe?

My watcher's eyes met mine—a flash of blue, a tongue of heat—before he pushed away from the wall, headed in my direction. I mumbled, "Be right back," to the detective and went to meet him. Moments later, the stranger and I faced each other, mere inches separating us. He towered over me, a mountain of a man who dwarfed my petite frame.

Everything receded, the noise, the smells, the emotional chaos. His face was a blur. All I saw, all I felt was the burn from eyes as blue as the Pacific Ocean, and as turbulent.

He cocked his head, confusion darkening those eyes.

An awakening inside me, where memories distant and terrible hid. My yearning reached for that, which was other in him, a harmonic resonance that sang a song I'd once intimately known, yet had long ago forgotten. Like electrons orbiting the same nucleus, we circled the source where that arcane otherness lived inside him. Inside me.

The melodic harmony intensified, my song rising in pitch, while his lowered, dancing wisps of melody, complementing, blending, to fulfill that perfect refrain.

The blue of his eyes became a sea as tears blurred my vision, the song's beauty devastating.

He gasped. Or maybe it was me.

"Agent Reese," a voice said.

I raised my hand to touch, to hold that song.

"Agent Reese!" repeated the voice.

I staggered, reluctantly turned my head at the sharp command.

Several feet away, the detective stared at me, frowning. "Are you all right?"

"Yes," I whispered.

I turned back once, just to confirm what my senses had screamed. The stranger was gone. So odd. I couldn't even describe his face.

"Sorry," I said to the detective when I reached him. "Where were we again?"

By the time the police released me, my watcher hadn't rematerialized, but pale echoes of the song stayed with me long after I left the Feed and Seed. I headed out to find Lulu when I caught my reflection in the rearview mirror. Blood all over me, crusted and drying. Crap. I dashed home, set *The Once and Future King* on my dresser, washed the blood off the Mylar, then showered and changed into jeans, a turtleneck, and a vest of my own knitting. I massaged my aching wrist. Thankfully, no damage.

Lucky me, Bernadette was at her weekly Wild Spaces meeting, and I peered out at a drab-gray afternoon sky, determined to get to Lulu fast. I collected my throwing knives, strapped them on, and slipped my small Bowie into its boot slot.

I shrugged into my barn coat, bent on doing a quick check on the animals, my basset Grace trotting behind me.

Frigging magic and chests? What was all Dave's woo-woo talk about? Was he hallucinating? Except Dave knew about the panther, as if he'd sent it to delay me, to save me. And that thing with my wrist felt real, too. I rubbed it. Let go. You could just tell when something was becoming a thing.

I stumbled—Dave Cochran, my protector, my mentor, my best friend. Truly gone. I caught myself and reached for the doorknob.

Bernadette materialized behind me, so fast, the pearl-handled derringer holstered at her waist flapped. It might not be loaded, but it packed a nasty wallop if she hugged me the wrong way.

"I thought you were out." My lips moved to tell her about Dave. I smothered the words. I couldn't give life to them. Not yet.

Her willowy form towered over me as she thrust a cup of yogurt-and-almonds at me.

"What?" I asked. "I don't need—"

"Eat." She stood in her fighter stance, legs akimbo, hands on knobby hips. "You don't get enough protein."

Gods. She was forever shoving food at me, as if being vegetarian equaled starvation. "I'm not hungry."

She harrumphed, slammed my yogurt onto the counter, and crossed her arms.

I picked up the cup and spoon. And here it comes, the bada-bum. There was always a bada-bum.

"Sit." Her grayed unibrow caterpillared when she pointed at the scarred Windsor chair beside the equally scarred pine table.

I remained standing, spooning the yogurt into my mouth. "I've gotta go, B."

"The captain called," she said.

Shit. "He's a special agent." A hell of an FBI agent, in fact, and aware Bernadette would answer the landline. Why had he called her? I slumped into the Windsor. "I'm returning to the Bureau on Monday, Bernadette. The doc signed off on me." I had to tell her about Dave. At some point.

She shook her head. "You're still fragile."

My ass. I smiled, projected comfort and reassurance. "I'm fine. And I'll be there on Monday, B. I need to work, to use my gifts. You've always told me that. I feel—"

"Too much, cookie. I know." She sat across from me and took my hand. "The captain's worried about you. Said so."

"Well, what the hell is he calling you for?" I stared into those knowing hazel eyes. "His worry… I don't like it. Look, I'm twenty-eight, not twelve. I'm plenty strong enough to swim those waters. I've done it for years."

She squeezed my shoulder. "Last interrogation, cookie, those waters drowned you."

"A one-off. It won't happen again." I glanced at my phone. Dammit. I had to get to Lulu. Now or never. "Dave's dead."

She closed those wise eyes, dropped her arms to her sides. Her hands fisted. "I know."

I enfolded her in a hug, and she hugged me back. A quick squeeze, gone in an instant. She stepped away, but I leaned in, kissed her parchment cheek. I turned and twisted the doorknob.

"Zut! There's more!" She followed me out the door.

"It can wait," I hollered back, my words watery with tears, as I strode to my car.

Effusive swearing in French tracked me.

A "something" pinged my mind. No, not a something. Someone. Bob. Bob? Nearby?

Was that what Dave meant by magic? No way. While Dave had honed my sensory abilities, I'd just been given a double dose of what everyone else had.

The crunch and whir of tires lacking purchase on our ice-coated drive broke the winter silence, inciting the birds to flight and my basset to howling. I scraped snow across my face, unwilling to let him see I'd been crying. Didn't want Bob knowing what a hot mess I was.

"Told you there was more, cookie!" Bernadette said. "Now buck it up."

Bob at the wheel. Another, too, in the car, an unfamiliar psychic scent. Feminine and strange.

An SUV crested the drive and skittered into the dooryard.

I so didn't need this right now.

The driver's door opened and Assistant Special Agent in Charge Bob Balfour emerged, his blue suit polished and immaculate, per usual. "Hey, Young Pup." His warm smile added wrinkles to his fifty-something face.

I walked over for a hug. "Hey, Old Man."

He puffed out his cheeks.

"What the hell are you doing here in New Hampshire?"

He adjusted his FBI lapel pin, grinned. "Couldn't stay away."

I snorted. "Yeah, like I'm buying that. You hate the country."

His brown eyes sparked with laughter. "Old dog, new tricks?"

"Waterfront in Arizona?"

A door slammed, and a whip-thin woman in a stylish parka minced around the SUV in three-inch heels. Heels? Really? She moved to Bob's left, all bangs-and-bunned hair and steel spine, except for her slightly askew black glasses, which annoyed me for no good reason.

She bobbed her head. "Sorry to interrupt, sir."

Bob gestured toward me. "Not at all. Clea, this is Special Agent Katie Taka, from Washington."

She held out her hand.

I tried to sense her, slammed against shields tighter than Bob's, artfully slithered around them, tasted. Ouch. She'd shoved me out, but I'd felt enough. Oily vibes.

"Nice to meet you," I said as we shook, wondering why Bob had brought her to the boonies to meet me. "Bob, I—"

A door slammed, and my foster mother stood on the porch, one hand on her hip, the other resting on the butt of her holstered derringer. No coat, no boots, she shook like an aspen.

"Clea!" Bernadette said. "Zut! Where are your manners? Bring them inside. I've got tea, coffee, and scones."

Oh, swellsies.

I took a step toward the house. Paused. A third presence? Over by the side of the barn, in shadow. Yes, a shadow, who waited and watched. I shuttered my lids and unfurled my mind.

The wash of hatred made me stumble back. But not at me, no. Directed at Taka and Bob. Vicious.

The shadow turned, lasered on me.

Concern, pursuit, determination encased in a shell of fierce protectiveness.

I drifted back toward the barn, as if I needed to check that the doors were closed tight. A pulse within the shadow, warm, inviting—it radiated sympathy and comfort and warmth. My mind stuttered. Was this the man with the song?

Adamantium shields slammed me backward, alerted by my clumsiness. Dammit. I raced to the barn, and found empty space and churned up snow. Not even a footprint.

"Clea?" Bob's hand on my elbow. "You all right?"

I hated when people asked me that. "Fine," I said.

The other. He'd stood there. That instant before he'd hardened his shields, I'd sensed fury, and that he'd come for me.

I should be alarmed.

Instead, I felt kinship.

We took over the living room. Me, in my worn red-leather chair, Grace curled at my feet, Bob and Taka across from me on the hideous plaid sofa that backed against the partition to the kitchen where Bernadette bustled.

I shoved Dave's death and finding Lulu aside, shored it up, at least until the grief breached those walls.

A relaxed Bob unbuttoned his jacket, smoothed his silver-and-brown hair, and I mentally searched for where I'd put the sticky dog brush to lift Grace's hair from his suit. The closet, maybe? The bath? Crap.

Taka scooched forward on the sofa. "I'm fascinated that you knit while you interrogate."

"Really," I deadpanned. Her insincerity was blatant. Maybe, I'd put the dog brush in kitchen tool drawer. Maybe, I won't offer it to her.

"Yes. So cozy."

I smirked. "That's me, cozy as Madame Defarge."

"Who?" she asked.

Gods. "My knitting's proven an effective tool."

"Your name is Clea," she said. "And yet your nickname? Another oddity. Do you like being called Sticks?"

For reals? "Years ago, my coworkers at counterintelligence thought it apt. I knit when I interrogated then, too. They didn't find it cozy in the least. It's spelled S-t-y-x, by the way. Like the river to Hades and death and, of course, like the knitting needles so useful as tools to disconcert perpetrators when I interrogate them. But I prefer Clea."

"Ah."

Her clueless act was bullshit. And her chilly demeanor would cripple her interrogation skills. She was a bad fit for that position. So why bring her to see me? Had to be one of Bob's frickin' arcane agendas. My warm smile countered hers. "You'll see it in action come Monday."

Bob cleared his throat.

I turned to him. "What?"

"How goes life on the farm?" he asked.

"Okay, Bob, fess up. Not that I'm not glad to see you, but what's the real deal, huh? Bernadette told me you'd called."

A soft chuckle. "Can't I even make pleasant chitchat first?"

"Sorry, Old Man. Of course, you can. It's just I've got stuff to take care of."

"I'm afraid you won't be back at the Bureau on Monday."

Continued...   ©Vicki Stiefel, 2017, Curiosity Quills Press

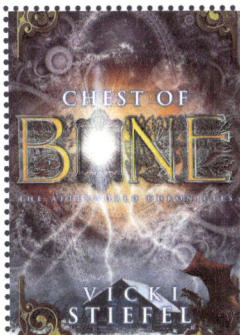

DEDICATION, ACKNOWLEDGEMENTS, AND COPYRIGHT

Dedicated to Magical Knitters Everywhere

ACKNOWLEDGEMENTS

Knit Photography by **Vicki Stiefel** (www.vickistiefel.com)

Steven Pisano, for Bernadette **(**https://www.flickr.com/photos/stevenpisano/)

Michel Curi, for Lulu (https://www.flickr.com/photos/119886413@N05/)

Curiosity Quills Press, (CuriosityQuills.com), *Chest of Bone* cover and excerpts

Eugene Teplitsky, designer (http://eugeneteplitsky.deviantart.com/), *Chest of Bone* cover

Helheimen Design, Cover Painting, Larrimer, and Clea: (HelheimenDesign.art.blog)

Designer and Author Images supplied by the individual designers and author

• *A very special "thank you!"* to **Henry Torossian, Kat Coyle** (https://thelittleknittery.com), and **Karen Clements** for showcasing our knitwear by modeling it so very well!

• *We so appreciate* **TIMES 10** (Times10.net), **Sarah**, and **Adam** for their design assistance.

• *A big nod* to the following yarn companies: **Illimani Yarn** for Clea's Vest • **Harrisville Designs** (harrisville.com) for Larrimer's Sweater • **Craftsy's Cloudborn Fibers** (www.craftsy.com/ideas/cloudborn) for Bernadette's Shawl, Mitts for Larrimer, and Lulu's Mitts

• *Finally, happy dancing that* **Jade Lee Lynch-Greenberg** put her sharp eyes on our manuscript to copyedit our pages.

COPYRIGHT

ISBN 978-0-9981242-1-6 (paperback)

www.ingramcontent.com/pod-product-compliance
Lightning Source LLC
LaVergne TN
LVHW072112070426
835509LV00003B/122